ALL-CLEAR

All-Clear

JOHN LATHAM

PETERLOO POETS

First published in 1990
by Peterloo Poets
2 Kelly Gardens, Calstock, Cornwall PL18 9SA, U.K.

British Library Cataloguing in Publication Data
Latham, John *1937– July 21–*
All-Clear.
I. Title
821.914
ISBN 1–871471–14–1

Printed in Great Britain by
Latimer Trend & Company Ltd, Plymouth

ACKNOWLEDGEMENTS are due to the editors of the following magazines in whose pages some of these poems first appeared: *Anglo-Welsh Review, Encounter, Giant Steps, Joe Soap's Canoe, The Literary Review, New Welsh Review, Orbis, Outposts, Poetry Durham, Poetry Matters, Poetry Review, The Rialto, Slow Dancer, Skoob Review, Staple, The Wide Skirt.*

'As I Lie Dying', 'Building a Library' and 'Exorcism' have been anthologised in *P.E.N. New Poetry 11*; 'Register' appeared in the *Lancaster Literature Festival Anthology*, 1986; 'The Lower Route to Strathy Bay' appeared in the *Lancaster Literature Festival Anthology*, 1989; 'Sakarta's Final Game of Go' appeared in *The National Poetry Society Competition Anthology*, 1986. An extract from the title poem, 'All-Clear', first appeared in *In Time of War* (Blackie).

'Bell', 'Sakarta's Final Game of Go' and 'Witch-Shooter' have been broadcast on *Poetry Now* (BBC Radio 3), and 'Witch-Shooter' was read on *Vision On.*

'Acrobats' won 1st prize in the *Manchester Open Poetry Competition*, 1989; 'Prompter' won 1st prize in the *Aberystwyth Competition*, 1986; 'Bell' won 2nd prize in the *Kent and Sussex Open Competition*, 1990; 'The Sinuosity of Coastlines and Rivers' won joint 1st prize in the *Anglo-Welsh Review Poetry Competition*, 1989; 'No Age at All' won 2nd prize in the *Staple Competition*, 1988; 'If We Move House' won 2nd prize in *Peterloo Poets Open Poetry Competition*, 1987; 'Sakarta's Final Game of Go' won 4th prize in the *National Poetry Competition*, 1986.

WITH THE ASSISTANCE OF

SOUTH WEST ARTS

Supported by

Cornwall County Council

Recipient of an Arts Council Incentive Funding Award

'For Harold Massingham
who opened this drawer
and showed me
why I can never close it.'

'Of the many people whose insights have helped improve the poems in this collection I wish particularly to thank the poets of "Off the Page": Margaret Guery, Jayne Hollinson, John Lyons, Marley Rose, John Ward and Chris Woods.'

Contents

The Day the Banana Cave was Sealed

'I want the banana cave. You must remember it!'
His toes would curl. Already
he was crawling
through its mellow shade, green light.

He'd mouth the words
a touch in front of mine
exaggerated, in case I should forget.

'I want the soup that Ernest drank
with buttercups and tadpoles'.
He'd wink at me and tap his head.

'Now the rope one, Daddy. But wait!
Wait until I've snuggled close'.
Eyes squeezed to hold the picture,
fists clenched to shut it out:
Tom, the captured bandit,
neck-noosed on a stool,
the sheriff nipping home, forgetting.

'Was he swinging when you found him?'
He'd nod his own reply,
hide his head inside my jumper.

He'd list the stories, plead for every one:
the cow that ate my sandals,
the sack Strider tied us in,
the Roman sandwich
I swapped for Ernest's bike,
the Easter camp when Mickey had no blanket
and crawled into the night to die.

For years, his passion nurtured them,
made them whole and true,
denied the staleness of each morning.

But now, as once again I plunge
through ferns and heather,
notch a willow for my bow,
I spot him in the mirror,
his lips aren't moving,
he winks at his friend and taps his head.

He sees me, smiles, eyes troubled.

A boulder rolls
across the entrance to the cave,
its green light deepens into darkness.

All-Clear

Miss Ryder is showing us how to breathe.
Eighteen of us, at triple desks,
in Mickey Mouse gas-masks, sad as cages,
mine smelling of my brother's rubber sheet'
my mother's still-warm shoes.
And in the yard, at playtime,
each mouse-face stretched to sorrow
at the top of every swing,
Ken Dykes and Chippy Fletcher slug it out,
crying quietly, unable to let go,
taking turns—impeccably—to strike.

'Underneath the spreading chestnut tree,
Mr Churchill said to me,
"If you want your gas-masks free
join the blinking A.R.P."

We loose our hands and scatter
to the far points of the yard
and Ernest Moon, as always,
squats behind a dinner-churn,
jersey pulled over his head.

The oil-lamp stutters in our air-raid shelter,
my father's massive shadow
enriching the dried roots of the turf above.
Mr Sutton blacks his face
with cork charred by the candle,
cleans his rifle with a plug of cotton wool.
'If Hitler lands at Frodsham
we'll trim his moustache at Barber Corker's',
he whispers through his emphysema.
I strain against the ventilation slit.
Smoke subdues the sky, in patches,
something large is rattling down the hill.
And the warning siren
halts the blurp of tugs on the canal.

My mother is ironing scraps of silver paper
we've saved for the wounded soldiers.
To patch their bullet-holes?
To make neat chimneys
for the smoke inside their bones
to flow more easily away?
To manufacture artificial limbs?
Mr Rigby hides his limp,
but when he leapt across the daffodils
to catch my green balloon
his left leg glinted in the sun.

The bomb crater up Fluin Lane is disappointin
cold, dry, no sign of blood,
no face-shapes blasted in the sand.
Too shallow, even, for the patient cow
who died last week in Mr Maddock's field
—sad, stiff-tailed, mourned by quiet flies.

Traitorous for handling
these shrapnel shards we swap at school,
their colour greasy to the touch,
we inspect our hands for warts
or grey stigmata.

Miss Ryder dips her ladle in the barrel,
tips chocolate powder
from our friends across the sea
into our tins and jars,
paper bags when these are full.
On Hillfields, after school,
behind our snail-race track,
we sniff, tongue it, gulp it down,
wonder if we'll ever breathe again.
Next week we give Ernest Moon
—who'd missed the gift through croup—
a jar of sand from Crowton quarry:
and we snort, bite knuckles,
as he slowly eats it, puzzled.

Who are these enemies with silly names,
beyond our tiptoed vision
even from the top of Frodsham Hill,
shapes tangled in the wireless hiss and crackle
when my father spins the yellow knob?
'That Mr Hitler. He's a fidget!',
said Miss Helsby when the firemen pulled her out.

'Oh Mr Churchill, what shall I do?
My cap blew off on Windy Rock
and floated down the brew.'

Walking, arms stretched, up my father's legs,
yet no closer to the stubble
that whiskers me to safety
when the dark's too quiet in my bed
—or to those lips that trumpet on my stomach,
my skin tingling
with self-willed, comb-and-paper pain.
The family comb, toothless as the piano
at which my mother, in her apron,
skims through 'Humoresque'.
The family toothbrush, curled, in a cracked cup
—how pretentious of the Bickerstaffs
in Bradley Lane, to have one each.

Waves of shade along the poker rammed into the fire.
Steam drifting from our cocoa, in tin mugs.

Sent to bed for telling God
not to bless my brother any more,
I stretch along the window-ledge,
and with my first real penknife
scratch a message in the paint:
'I lived a buggar life in this house'.
Two years later, my mother finds it, cries.

'Sticks and stones may break my bones
but words will never hurt me'.

Untying knots in haybag string,
kneeling on rough concrete with my wooden hammer,
straightening nails,
not bringing flowers called 'mother die'
into the house.
'Undying love',
inscribed on the stone slab
which will cover Uncle Tommy
when they find him,
bring him home from France.
In the meantime
he shelters on the mantelpiece, at Auntie Lou's,
among his family of prizes
for rifle-shooting at Silcock's Easter fair
—clay figures, bright maroon,
which make fine white powder
when I scratch their undersides.
A boy soldier, Adam's apple scared,
as though he were foreseeing
my mother and my aunt,
tight around each other, rocking slow,
while a telegram drowns
in water from the overspilling sink.
They look so small.

Run a stick along the palings, shoot them dead.

'Forty years on, when afar and asunder',
we bellow at the floor,
while Pardy flicks a water-bomb
at girls across the aisle,
old Shelley, at the piano,
swiftly dabs his eye,
and the sun, through a tall window,
makes the dust-motes yawn.

Pale concentric rings
of a torch in hand-cupped blackout.

The bluebell promise of our willow-pattern plate,
survivor of the wedding set,
reserved for pilchard sandwiches
when Auntie Doris comes for tea.
Polish in the creases of the interwoven petals
on the sideboard door
holds my fingernail's fine arc
until I count to thirty five.
Its smell, locked to the surface,
is Ascension Day at church,
and my nostril clouds that dull its sheen
fade from the outside in.

The all-clear siren loops again,
teasing sturdy tugs on the canal.
The street is dancing.
'Your whole self in, your whole self out,
in out, in out, shake it all about'.
Mrs Calveley sags against the trestle table,
and Anne and I, forgotten, hiding underneath,
inch the white cloth lower on the dancers' side,
our jellies and blancmanges
reflecting coloured lights
strung from house to house across the road.
Sticky fingers to each other's lips
we watch disembodied legs
whirl or sombrely slide by:
Mr Fawkes, no socks inside his polished boots,
Mrs Turner, thicker at the ankle than the thigh,
no knees,
Miss Gill's silk stockings snailed with glue
—to stop her overflowing on the road?
Anne's hand is warm,
her blouse breathes as she sleeps,
her face stroked green and yellow,
blue, then green again.
Floating on my hammock, on the Good Ship Lollipop,
I watch the lights grow dim,
sink beneath the lowland sea.

Hitler, rakish in a green bow-tie,
cast-off morning suit of Mr Capper's,
steel swastika sewn on his lapel,
is stoically burning,
aloof, almost forgiving,
while we clap and cheer,
and his moustache melts
in a sudden spear of flame
from his torn trouser-leg.
Why does Mrs Waterman,
husband missing since the year the war began,
not jeer or shout hooray
as Hitler loses balance,
topples gravely, top-hat first,
into the crazy nest of flame
—but instead, draws Vic,
my next-best friend,
into her coat, and turns away?

We trawl the embers in the morning.
I lift Hitler's shrivelled gas-mask
with my stick: it leers.
Ernest pounces, screams,
writhes on the grass.
We open his tight fingers
—a swastika, burned into his skin.

Witch-Shooter

Sam's gone home. I'm kneeling, sweeping nails:
his witch-shooter, forgotten, on its side
—a test for urban archaeologists, already.

Before he came, I'd a workshop in my cellar,
but under his ranging, uncompromising eye
it gathered light and shade, became a cave,
damp-walled, breathing: holy as we crept
past Granny in the hamper, counting toes,
deepening as he stared up through a grille,
showed me the remoteness of a leaf-fringed sky.

Cobwebs, their shadows, my miscellany of tools
decided him— he'd make a witch-shooter.
It grew fast under his hammer. The bobbin
swivelled on the block of varnished pine,
the broken coat-hanger pivoted and scanned:
tongue-furled, eyes-screwed concentration,
painting it and his trouser-knees white.

He explained its working. It fired no bullets,
shed no blood, no witches were exterminated,
crippled. All it did was weave a skirt
into whose folds they could not follow.
When he heard his mother's voice he swelled,
told me how strong he was at nailing.
When her footsteps faded, he sucked his thumb.

Sam's gone home. He'll come again if Mummy says.
He's left his thumbprint on the bobbin.
I'm in the cave, sweeping nails and whistling.

If We Move House,

I won't see again those discs of coloured light
skating gravely round my wall, or find comfort
in the cupboard that turns drab blankets gay,
where I hide, feed my spider if Mr Ruhnke comes,
smell my father on this towel he used to rub,
dab, wipe, saw, flick me dry—and then himself.

My mother doesn't smell of lazy stories anymore;
only her teeth smile now. She hugs me clumsily
—serpent brooch screwed hard into my face—
cries inside her if I wince. When I tricked her
with the hollow egg she just looked puzzled:
Mr Ruhnke frowned, then smiled and crunched it.

In the dream I often have that always soaks me
I drag my father to her, but she floats away,
I tug her to his bedside, but he won't wake up
—turned into a trunk. The only one who knows
how to soap my yellow boat to stop it listing:
why I'm scared to watch the water swirl away.

He's still here if I sift the lines of fluff
along the skirting, rummage deep into the back
of his scorched chair, trawl the shadow-spaces
underneath their bed, where the mattress sags
and sadly breathes—and last week Mr Ruhnke
left those fancy shoes he'll never see again.

A matchbox full of dead ones curled together,
a crumpled note: 'Your dinner's on the stove',
the conker I lent him for his trip to Trinidad,
snippings from his hair, and hers, his pouch
that smells of sleep, glass from his old watch
—it makes my thumbprints twist the other way.

Journey to the Promised Land

Her eyes gape, drink everything in.
She whirls at roof-space rustling,
chimney's breath. Hand-grip tightens
at a lamb's 'Find me' from the night.
Quietened by centuries, stone walls
her arms-span thick, she whispers.
Not even the dead mouse in the bath
provokes a cry: simply a blanching.

Dawn. Her shrieking scythes my sleep.
Scalded? Savaged by the farmer's dog?
I hurtle to the shrillness drilling.
A finger gibbers at the kitchen wall,
scattershot with woodlice, plump
on winter's damp: a charnel smell.
I kneel, envelop her, taste salt.
Her screams subside into my chest.

The creatures have to leave. But only
when she's built new homes for them,
a village on the far side of the field,
with oyster-shells for beds and baths,
onion-flavoured crisps for hibernation.
And only when they've all been named,
all ninety-three, Crown Prince Sean
down to Dirk, the hunch-backed slave.

Brush-flipped from the wall, tipped
with tongue-extended care into a pail,
sugar sprinkled on, in case of hunger,
they're carried careful as a candle
from shadow into sunshine, stuttering
a trail through swiftly drying grass:
girl and grateful woodlice singing,
swinging gently to the promised land.

'All God's children . . .' I smile
at the butterfly resting on my spade.
Seeds float . . . Squeals skewer me.
'Forgive me, Sean!' On the skyline
ribboned pigtails, one red, one blue,
caper, juggling the sun. My daughter,
weeping, her eyes imploring Heaven,
stamping on the woodlice in the pail.

Something I Daren't Lose

You've been dead almost a day,
and still my feet are bleeding.

When I saw you, rumpled,
hidden in the grass,
wing flailing
half-hinged door,
beak straining
issuing no sound,
I knew I'd save you.

When I lifted you
your heart raced,
but as I whispered
stroked you
you quietened,
stopped calling,
lay easy on my hand.

It was the threads
sliding—yellow,
laced with red—
sucking from you
a summer full of song,
sucking through my skin
something I daren't lose.

You've been dead almost a week,
and still my feet are stamping.

Listening to the Dark

Her shrill voice scissors me awake.

Tiptoed at the window,
she's shivering so hard
her cot jigs across the floor.

'Killer ants', she whispers
finger stabbing at the dark.
Only her slide, upturned for painting.

'They're creeping close!'
Just a kitten
stretching on the garden wall.

'I can hear them sucking juices'.
Only the breeze,
lapping at the willow.

'Listen to the dark!'
I stroke her into slow thumb-sucking,
sink towards my cornfield dream.

. . . . . .

Sky pouring
through the open window,
the dark a stethoscope.

A car slowing
on the hill up to Long Marton,
the driver hesitant, changing gear.

Feathers rustling
as a pigeon veers to starboard,
homing late.

Thud of a cow's tail onto grass
warmed by its body
softened in the mist.

Swish of a snail,
drawing up its skirts
against the dew.

Shudder of an oak-tree
scored by claws—a fledgling
trying to correct its balance.

A blind dog sniffing
round cemetery stones,
drunk with history.

Caterwaul of sirens on the Ship Canal,
a kettle seething
somewhere in Long Marton.

From the tower, each quarter,
the fussy buzz of wheels
caught almost napping:

then, clear strokes, echo-loops,
high notes sponged by mosses
on the lych gate's northern face;

the sigh of dust
settling once again
into a different pattern.

A spider swelling. Its fly
flapping at the seamless moon
is still half-full.

Killer-cats padding the garden wall,
clawing up the ivy,
slinking underneath the sash.

Topsy

He shivers, beckons from deep shadow,
brow mirroring the tailored grass
still glassed with dew in afternoon.

His jacket droops now, looser, baggy,
his pockets sag with matches, string,
skeletons of things, a ring of washers.

She hesitates in sunshine, staring:
her buckle flares, gold igniting blue
as she stubs her shoe into the turf.

This man can't be her grandfather,
who gathered flowers, climbed trees,
his knees a mountainside, a saddle.

Something—his awkwardness, perhaps—
unwraps her. She smiles, waves, skips,
dips into a sprint, dew flying.

Gaps between her footprints widen,
while deep inside his ragged memory
he, in buttoned shoes, is running, too.

She leaps into his halting space:
a blur of lace, red ribbons, thighs,
and rising slow, her overturning skirt.

He topsies her, this final time, sways,
delays the darkness rushing, winces,
grins as she spins round to her mother.

Beethoven's Opus 130

Swifter than the global winds
his cavatina scythes
through market-places, fractured minds,
valleys stunned by sun or months of snow,
two hundred years, and more,
since he first sucked solace
from the painful air; and in the square
a woman twirls her handbag,
a girl remembers her lost night,
an old man frowns, sucks harder on his pipe.

Six people—eight at most—
all within the shadow
of a shallow sandstone hill,
twist their lips, this morning,
into cavatina smiles,
on a man's first birthday without breath;
ears jogged once again
by those ash-voiced stories
that would vanish written down,
and are sinking now:
while my mother, lost in music,
takes two teacups from the rack
—and slowly puts one back.

Somewhere, perhaps, at milking-time,
a thousand years ago,
a girl was born in straw,
and long before the vapour
had ceased rising from the pail,
a youth shivered at that falter in her voice,
which, frayed, softened
by the generations' glide,
edged the cavatina's quaver,
my father's burr
—and still may halt a breath or two
in Adelaide or fevered dreams.

No Age at All

'Wait until I'm older than you.
Just wait'.
His arms-length
greater than my kicking-range,
and when my legs had flailed
into exhaustion
he'd draw me in.
I'd hear his heart deep thumping,
slowing mine to his
—and for that moment
before he set me down
I was no age at all.

I'm catching up on him.
My second birthday
since his slack heart stuttered,
tightened,
forgot,
and he moved forever
out of kicking-range,
words he couldn't find
not needed—never were—
that moment
he tried to draw me down,
became no age at all.

Doing for You Now

He frowned as I told them, scraped soil
off his boots, slowly leaned his spade
against the wall. She stood cumbersome,
face fixed. Only her hands betrayed,
massaging her worn knuckles, as once
they'd soothed her children, frightened
in large beds. She fumbled in her apron
—shapes of clothes-pegs surfacing—
her eyes grew old, she swallowed hard,
'But Son. Son. Who'll do for you now?'

She did for him, for almost fifty years,
her fingers swelling as he thinned,
and with soups and rich milk puddings
withdrew from the table, to the fireside,
up the stairs. She would have eased him
inch by inch through babyhood or madness
if he'd lived. 'It's not him now', palm
wandering his frozen face, immaculate.
Her voice steady on their anniversary,
then the telephone clattering like teeth.

But now her grand-children make legends
of thickly crusted pies she can't tell us
how she bakes, their knife-fork chatter
kneads the dough again. She darns clothes
from my old marriage: stitching coarser
but still strong. Standing heavily today,
when I brought my friend to meet her,
and a chapped hand squeezed a slim one,
found warmth that answered yes, her face
shed years, she smoothed her apron down.

Exorcism

On each one of the years of nights since then
—when he forced himself from coma,
stared around the room, milk-blind,
failed to find us, strained
until he snapped back, dead—
I've squeezed my eyes, willed him into view.
He's come reluctantly, distorted, never whole:
a fragment of his forehead, an elongated chin,
a mocking grin he never had,
loose-cobwebbed eyes.
In those thousand nights, he never smiled.

Perhaps it was your fingers' music as we talked,
or seeds gliding all ways past our window. Today,
strangers, for an hour, in mottled space,
from half-dreams and our ignorance,
we shaped a vision, shared it
—a bubble, floating, sloughing violet and green,
a ladybird inside it, swollen by the lens,
sliding down a curved slope—trapped;
the bubble wobbling in the slip-stream of a wing,
bursting in a cataract of stars;
a red bead lifting, swirling off. As you left,
your smile was from inside the bubble.

Tonight he was lying in a field, intact,
face open to the sun, which chased a ladybird
deep into the caverns of his hair
—now brown again.
He rocked onto his elbow, and as he smiled at me
his fingers traced the full length of a straw,
lingered at a knot,
untying it. He smoothed its creases out,
tucked it in the grass. For a moment
his smile hung, huge above my cot.
His darkness is completed; I can sleep.

Register

The smell of ink-wells, chalks.
Four decades since she closed the desk
from which, on a high stool,
she pencil-tapped us through the register,
the five-times table, enjoined us
not to peep through fingers during prayers:
Miss Hutton. A hundred now, the paper says.

Her room, violet as her wrists.
She sits stiff-backed, by a quiet fire,
needles trembling slightly
like the hollow ruler—ebony we thought—
before it rapped against the blackboard
or our knuckles, tense in her cool hand.

The same crisp voice—though weaker—
the gaze that made us lower our eyes.
But she can't place me.
Or Jane, kicked through the railings
by the coalman's horse,
or the day Sam Abel sneezed his gas-mask off.
'Too long ago', she grumbles, pouring tea.

Suddenly her needle jabs the dust-motes.
'Yes! Now I see you at that angle, in the sun'.
And she reminds me how, one winter,
I brought her a potato, piping hot,
how she caught me nudging snails along my slate,
and how, when my mother died, I painted weeds.

But she's trawled in deeper water than she thought.
It is not I, but my father,
resurrected, back to childhood,
on this afternoon of seed-cake and frail china.
She's dozing now, lightly as a child.
Eyes closed, Miss Hutton. Eyes closed, young Jack.
No peeping.

Building a Library

(for Marcia Baker)

They take up little space—grandfather, brother, father—
together on your shelf:
your fingers stroke them—vellum, paper, cloth.

Kneeling at a box, you raise him, leaf by brittle leaf:
certificates in long-hand
from college in Odessa, the Emperor's seal, cracked wax.

You translate slowly—lingering with the whorls, loops,
mottled curlicues—
you coax him into view. Not the trim white-bearded man

who tossed you to the sky, tramped fields with you,
but a hob-nailed youth
huddled on a boat, shivering, trying to strain west.

The mist through which you see him mutes his colours,
thins the texture of his voice,
the way he fashioned stories with eyebrows, hands,

—as slender, I suspect, as those resting on the box
as you blow old dust away, say
'If he could open these he'd be engulfed in visions'.

Your fingers, delving, shuffle latin, algebra. And air
trapped in Odessa, in 1882,
rises through your window, floats off to Puget Sound.

It is time to put the box away. Perhaps in twenty years
a fourth book will be written,
by a girl who frowns like you, inclines a pen like him.

The fog will have thickened. It should be enough for us
to sense a distant scuffle,
which might be boots on planking—or a poker in the ash.

Ocean Song

This fragment of a shell crushed by a mastodon,
lifted from the valley floor by foehn,
has been settling through my stillness
since the last ice-tongues slid away.

My darkness gathers, extends the sense of touch.
How the flatfish throb
as they slide across each other,
face to face!

Turtles crawl into my skin to cool their shells,
I suck slow poisons from the sky.
And when my ancient ones—the whales—
seek sanctuary in fissures, fresh-melt caves,
I beat, spume to keep them warm.

Stories in the layers of dust that cloak my bed:
swollen in the comet years,
thin when you grew cold,
yellow when the wayward star burned up.

When the crust beneath me yields,
mountains move up through me,
bubbles large as icebergs
—emerald, flecked with bats—
thresh their way to freer air above.

When I'm tired I shrug, brush wasps away.
Or I drink you in, breathe mist,
obliterate myself, swallow my own rain.

You draw me out all day,
but at night the slow earth pulls me back.

We are quiet, both.
But your silence seethes. Mine waits.

If a wandering rock invades you,
you rip it, spit it out.
I open, swallow it whole.

I'll still live after you've blazed away:
my fertility, in grains and wisps of straw,
locked into the ice—faint discolorations,
specks in the interstices, waiting for the thaw.

I cradle your bright child each day,
at night take it to rest
while you yawn, paint pictures in the sky:
throat-colours of thin fish
in my deepest parts.

You, the sire: those crimson seeds
that rain on me all day.
It is in me they grow,
from me that some stumble, dripping, to the shore,
prints fading—no glance behind.
But I take my children back, in time,
enfold again the galleons
tall wood—cracked and tired—
from forests nurtured by my early morning breath.

The sting of hail, a log's slow twirl,
bees that surf the breakers in the night,
thud of dead birds from the convoy winging south.
All skin-deep.

Underneath I am orderly and cold,
stirred only by the fishes' sideways wobble
—each trapped within its level,
a billion skins, thinning as your light fades out:
and from time to time by whales.
Inside my stillness
we listen to each other's pain.

I long for the shadow of a pterodactyl's glide.

Homing

What chance this nest of sparks,
swirling out of flames
into the chimney's night,
swooping for the cold-eyed wind,

will find beyond this reckless sky
the star that spawned it,
nurtured it through fire
into a cloak of nervous leaves,

a sturdy branch that breathed,
until a saw, a smell of wax,
a quiet time, an axe, a match
—this recent restlessness?

Prescription for a State of Harmony

Find a quiet spot to build a tower of stones
perhaps beside a stream
for water-smoothed ones.
The ground need not be flat.

Select, discard them with respect.

Kneel, cup each one in your hands.
To find its proper angle
breathe its dust away, turn it:
when it balances, you'll know.

As you ease it into place
notice how it pulls,
binds to the others.

All shapes and sizes are allowed.
You shouldn't be afraid
to place jagged ones low down:
the tower can touch you
only if it's close to toppling.
Better still, be frightened:
but hold your breath
and do it, even so.

When it's tall enough
shelter in deep ferns,
watch as sunlight
throughout the afternoon
slides across its modesties.

When it's time
touch it with a grass.
You'll scarcely hear it falling.

Imagine, as you walk away,
how turf will grow, sheltering the stones.

Bell

No-one was quite sure how or when it cracked,
the mechanisms failed
—or when ivy clogged the arrow-slits,
spiders wove a carpet on the twisting sandstone steps,
starlings started nesting in the dome.

At last he saw the damage: he bowed his head.

He chose old tools, because he wanted the memories
of frayings, flaws, uneven textures to the grain.

He worked in subdued light, so the wood wouldn't warp
in the harshness of the sun,
the glue not dry too quickly and be brittle.

He plaited hemp by hand, seeking the old tension,
roughness, elasticity.

Sometimes stooped or bending back, often on his knees,
he used pumice, birch-twigs, beeswax,
thorns of gorse;
logs to fuel the furnace, so the heating would be slow.

Eschewing rivets, nails,
pins harder than the sections to be joined,
he carved pegs from pear and willow,
tapped them home with a hammer wrapped in hide.

Soft metals, leather, rope—he fashioned all new parts
so they would ease into their ageing.

The old bell had been stamped with his initials, date:
he smoothed them out—no markings on the iron.

Not as finished as before: perhaps a slight distortion
from the crack. But mellow, modest, whole.

He tied the ivy back to let in filtered light,
draped fronds of it and wind-stirred leaves
to mute the stark lines of the windows.

He knelt, hesitated, stretched to pull the rope.

He felt wheels and pulleys turn,
cogs slide into place,
percussion of the ball against the dome:
he felt the bell swing, falter,
and in the swelling silence
the stones of the tower, absorbing sound.

And as starlings rose from a grove of distant elms,
the bell drew richness from the walls,
gained confidence and warmth. It glowed. It sang.

Apple Gatherers

(after Stanley Spencer)

If you put those whips away
the stiffness in our arms would disappear,
we could open wider, gather more.

You don't need to starve our elders,
too weak, confused, to pluck.
Let them suck the bruised ones

lying in the grass;
they do no harm, and their years
gather us like apples, keep us calm.

Our stunted children cannot reach the fruit,
but their ears are quick
to catch the rattle of its ripeness.

Though we have no letters we have wisdoms.
Always leave some hanging
to remind the trees of Spring;

the finest apples grow almost at the top
where leaves protect them from the sun,
but they're open to the moon's more subtle light;

firm ones floored by gales
should be coracled in grass,
left to ripen, floating in a stream.

The backlash of your whips must hurt you.
Cast them to the grass,
press your faces to our harvest, dream.

We would not flee. If a few should wander off
to fish the coastal waters
their children would come back to gather apples.

Prompter

I've made this pit into my home.
Stool with horse-hair cushion,
scripts all neatly stacked,
hammock slung between the joists,
brazier for tea and rabbit stew.

Great actors are outlaws,
flawed and fancy-free.
They don't need to see me,
they move to my faint shadow
when I frown or shake my head.

When blindness came
I learned to finger-scan the scripts
and soon could palm whole sections
if I tuned my skin with wax.
No need now to light my candles.

Great actors are children,
light with memories,
each opening of the curtain a new day.
If they race into the sun too fast
I tap the stage to make them falter.

Now I'm almost deaf, I guage pace
from flexing of the boards.
Today I fell asleep in 'Uncle Vanya'.
Thank God there's just one story
—different tellings.

Great actors are ghosts,
bringing us new visions
from days of rush and quill.
They don't need to hear me. Enough
to know I'm with them, mouthing.

The Lower Route to Strathy Bay

If Miss McWaters, in her shift,
is peeping through the curtains
of her sunken hut,
you mustn't see her wave
—smile to yourself
as though the sun has just come out.

Nod to Mr Potter,
who'll be tapping out his pipe
against the garden wall.
If his rhythm is 'Pop the weasel'
skip along the kerbstones,
pale green sparks—and hurry on.

When you pass the roofless chapel
try not to frighten
the thin man tangled in the vine.
Try not to notice
how his toes are the colour
of roots they've knotted round.

Scratch on the bottom
of the upturned boat,
warm your hands against the chimney,
breathe the sorrel in its smoke,
call 'Good morning, Mrs Boxer'
—but don't stop.

And if the old man fishing
from the milestone by the brook
is facing the wrong way,
take off your shoes and tiptoe
trying not to splash
—breathing like a fish.

A Truly Global Curry

Winds lap the spinning Earth in twenty days, he read, move faster
higher up. That, being jilted, and the traffic jams, decided him.
He'd spend his holidays this year at the skylight of his attic,
and winds would bring scents from everywhere: flowers of Africa;
volcanic smouldering; mushrooms swelling in Venezuelan groves;
pearls whitening under sun; lilies motionless in Arctic pools;
seeds bursting on braziers in Singapore, cracking in the bush;
fear welling from the sites of prehistoric battles: much more.

He slung a hammock underneath the barefaced glass, set pillows
so his nose poked through. In a hanging basket: ships biscuits,
a commode, dried apricots, a salt-block, towels to soak up rain.
He carved an alabaster shield to protect his nose from sunlight,
pigeons flying low. He lashed his ancient atlas to the ceiling,
used Newton's laws to plot the winds. At dawn, on the first day,
he dabbed the breeze with camphor. It would circuit in two weeks,
precisely. His nose quivered. He stretched and closed his eyes.

Daylight hours were useless. Too many local fumes: chip-shops,
traffic, tar in Market Street, birds that perched upwind of him
to fart. So he travelled just at night, and in a swelling moon
sailed west through Obdarak, dipped down to Turkestan, Skejansk.
Reception faded—almost lost by Lhasa—so he tuned his nostrils
by pinning them with iron in a lodestone collar, to fix his angle
to the core. Japonica, in waves. But a starling started nesting
in his nasal hair. Sneezes made him overshoot the Wrangell Isles.

He lost weight, colour, on his holiday; only his nose was bronzed.
But as he crossed the final tract, and found that by swivelling
he could scan a full radian of latitude—the smells more vivid,
richer all the time: red-eyed beans from Arkansas, moist leaves
from Martinique—he decided the world is broader from a hammock,
the winds more powerful than steel. As he dropped onto the floor
and sniffed, he realised Miss Viswanath, from next-door-but-two,
made truly global curry—not a hamlet or a coral reef left out.

Poet Reclining in the Grass

(after Chagall)

They missed the hyphens out.
I'm not a poet, free to move about,
meandering the meadows,
watching dragonflies glide past
into a vale of aching mist:
I'm a poet-reclining-in-the-grass.

I've been forced into this role.
They might as well have dug a hole
and staked me down. I don't ask much, I'm quiet,
cleanly dressed and mild,
but I'm spillage from a palette,
M. Chagall's lost night; his cuckoo child.

I have two friends, albino pig and horse.
Pig nuzzles me and tells about the boars
she used to know, snuffles, snouts me cool
when the sun scorches my skin:
and if the wind disturbs my blouse
she smoothes it with her jowls, and tucks it in.

Horse snorts, watchful at my side.
He shelters me from rain, kneels to ride
the blizzards while I thaw against his flanks;
and when birds of prey swoop low,
he straddles me and bristles,
shadowing my body, top to toe.

They come to me at sundown, wait,
and I talk to them of prairies, streams in spate,
mud-pools bubbling, the smell of western pines.
We're joined by field-mice, foxes—once, an ass—
and my words glow in the half-light:
I'm a poet, now, reclining in the grass.

As I Lie Dying

We skirt the Vistula, piggy-back tired tumbleweed
in Yoknapatawpha County, inhale the smell of words
and whelks in old O'Connell Street, slink along
St Petersburg's stone flags. My face is brushed
by Sonya's fingers, I breathe her sackcloth hair,
but Lebedyev is tugging me, her glove flies free,
she recoils into a doorway, and on the lantern's
faint horizon she is swallowed by the damp cloak
of a pock-marked general. At an upstairs window,
Pierre, in heavy spectacles, wrestles with a bear.

A month at most, the doctor said. The bookshelves
in my drifting head are crammed. No space to make
new friends—a time for family: they stir, begin
to mill. I flounder through my fever, but the wind
has veered again, mist hissing, curtaining my eyes.

Tressilian, straw-sandalled, stiffly at the door:
a large room, vague with smoke and muted laughter,
Mrs Gamp and Lebedyev careering round with trays.
Vardaman spills mead on Mr Knightley, hypnotised
by Catherine's white whip. The quartet strikes up:
Maggie Tulliver's drowned toes paddling ballads
in bowls of shallow water, Huck rocking his barrel
to the plaint of Castorp's punctured throat, Flay
dictating tempo with the cracking of his knees,
echoing from conch-shells on the onyx chandeliers.

Outside, those great unread, whom I am spurning:
not a burning of the books, just an abandonment
to fresher libraries. My friends gather, populate
the shifting dark with movement, voice and shade.
How disorderly they are: how blurred and intimate.

Tull whirrups the mule along the Nevsky Prospect,
pawns Nastasya Filippovna, sheathed in concrete,
ankles turning green. 'Now I can git them teeth',
Prince Myshkin cries. A small boy sucks a mirror,
a clown weeps in his bath. Molly swirls her skirts
around Giles Winterborne: Oskar is soft-drumming
underneath with K. Sonya beckons from the shadows
of an alley, her hand thinned almost to the bone.
Where our wrist-skins touch it burns with fever.
But Lebedyev is tugging at me—tugging very hard.

Sakata's Final Game of Go

This smooth stone between my fourth and middle fingers
hangs above the board,
divines the perfect shape, swoops
onto the chosen cross. It clicks, quivers,
lost in a fresh landscape of white and black.
My toes tighten in my slippers.

Cross-legged on the mat,
I wait for Takagi's wrist to rise.
Sunlight splays through a chink in the bamboo,
softens pinks and yellows in the thin silk
stretched between my knees,
loose above the deep pain in my stomach,
where purple stones are sprouting every day.
Soon I will scald my knife eleven times.

I am riding a horse, up to its shoulders in fine sand.

In all our years of fighting
I have never seen his face
—just his tense wrist
as the silk slips back
before his stone descends,
the vein that pulses if the shape made is joseki.
That is often, now.
He has served his apprenticeship,
mastered the eye-stealing tesuji.

No time left for scuffles in the corner,
I move where the rivers have wide curves.
Beyond food now, I need only boiling water,
green powder in a patterned bowl:
porcelain calm as the opal on my mother's ring.

Takagi's fingers tremble. His vein swells,
begins to throb. My tongue
finds the jagged tooth and presses twice,
his stone's swift click rips across my eyes.
There is death in the ha-ne; the proverb is fulfilled.

The clouds of sand stop swirling, settle to the floor:
the trees ivory, no leaves.

I, Sakata Eio, bow three times,
take my mind between my fourth and middle fingers,
fold it small, place it to the side,
cover it with silk.

Solo Climb

He hangs, one-handed, beginning not to care,
from this silver birch that broke his fall,
no feeling in his other arm, lips cracked
through lack of rain: the tree a miracle,
the only green, sprouting from a crevice
in granite, five hundred feet from ground.

At times, her face in distant tussocks,
scudding clouds: swollen, weeping quietly.

He's cooling. Snowflakes landing on his skin
no longer melt. Ice has braceleted the bark
below his hand. Frictionless, a pendulum,
he swings over in the gales, looks down
on ravens' footprints patterning the branch,
a smoke-thread curling from his cottage.

No way to reach the chocolate in his pocket:
his only food, since he slipped two days ago,
the moth that dazed him with its dancing,
curtseyed, fluttered, settled on his chin.
His sinews harden. Soon his wrist will snap,
the sapling, shedding diamonds, spring back.

A seed balancing the thermal beckons him.
He understands. He wills a surge of blood
to flood his fingers, thaw them. He shrugs,
lets go. He floats, his cape a parachute,
the earth glowing as it climbs to greet him,
skaters on the lake performing pirouettes.

Almost down, washed by vapours from the bath
she's drawn for him, he smells bacon frying,
hears ice cubes cracking in his whisky-glass.
She's waving to him. Her smile is everywhere.
Her lips push forwards, swollen, weeping.
They part to swallow him. He arches, flails.

His hand flicks granite, he claws the cliff,
his boots steady on a thimble of dry stone.

He breathes deeply, won't look down again,
presses his face against the rock, tastes it.
He loves its coolness, texture of its skin.
He's not hungry now. Toehold to his right,
a cleft to wedge his fist in, teeth intact,
he starts to climb, one-handed: sky opening.

Protection from Dragons

You remember, Father, how willingly I took her in,
how I rejoiced when she taught my child cat's cradle,
lulled him with those stories that used to soften me?
I'd knead or knit downstairs, soothed by the music
of the oldest tones I know and the fascinated new.
The shrinking of her memory seemed natural, somehow.
But not to her, Father! Those losses made her wild.
She smashed china, scorched the bird: and the night
I came in early, saw my son's thin arms, that always
had stretched up to me—then to her—for solace,
curved into a shield that could never hope to parry
hen-peck chopping from hands that used to shelter me
from dragons, I knew she had to go: to save my child,
not so much from punches as bewilderment. Forgive me.

Who is it, Holy Father, whose smile I used to know,
who stuffs coals into my mouth: forces me to laugh
into my pain—laugh, or she'll take the tongs again?

Touch me, Father, through the grille. Just as you did
when I wore ribbons. Then I'll know you understand.
She's in a home where everybody's memory is failing,
so each day she makes new friends. I've discovered
how to ease the pain of visiting. I bring a basket
of jalopena peppers. When I've hugged, buttoned her,
she's pleased and puzzled, I pop one in her mouth.
She bites it, gasps, turns crimson, sweat-beads swell,
but when I laugh, Father, she starts laughing, too,
rocking in her chair, tears streaming. In a minute
she forgets, fidgets, frowns. I pop another pepper in,
she chews, we laugh. So we're merry for the whole hour
of my visit. At the bell, I kiss her, put ointment
on her lips. She's fine, Father. Touch me once again.

Who is it, Holy Father, who takes these liberties:
who, just because I've seen her eyes in mirrors,
forces me to laugh, to deny the tongues of dragons?

Fluted Vase

The bell reverberates around your empty house,
I wrap rags round my feet, sneak in.

I pad from room to room, nuzzling your shoes,
curling loose hairs on your jacket into ovals.

Sitting on a hard chair in the darkest corner
I picture flame-pools in your glasses as you read.

I smooth your sheets, trying not to think
of dreams that could cause those creases, tears.

I press your pipe-bowl to my forehead:
sometimes a little warmth returns.

I thrust my head inside your laundry chest,
drink—eyes closed—until the air turns green.

Squinting, cheek against the bathroom wall,
I search the mirror for your dragon-breath.

I finger crevices your nails make in the soap,
smooth them over, mark them with a kiss.

I pour a little water
in the fluted vase that holds dry flowers.

Last of all, I turn your pillow over,
hiss at the photograph smiling by your bed,

I suck your toothbrush, suck it dry,
sneak away as your key turns in the lock.

Whetstone

At the blind end of the larder, behind the broken shelves,
I find our whetstone, bullrush-smoothed by dust.

Lighter than it seemed when you last flourished it,
carving-knife flamboyant,
dicing vapour-riddled air,
slicing through our voices in the 'Twelfth Street Rag'
and the firm cap of your finger, delicately crooked,
gentle splash into the broth;
you laughing at my scream, writing 'I love you'
scarlet on my flour-coated wrist: fainting.
That evening, by candle-light—your bandage
humbly blessing—we ate it lightly fried, with rosemary
and thyme. 'Good but somewhat rubbery', you said.

Through fifty years of nights
your knees were whetstones to the soft flesh
behind mine. So now, each evening,
I warm two oranges beside the fire,
scuff them with a match-box to the texture of your skin
and in bed curl on my side, press them into place.
It is usually dawn before the heat has slipped away.

And in the same lost corner, your crumpled working shirt,
patched where the coil of wire sprang back.
If I soak it in hot water could I taste your youth again?
You stride in, urgent, from threshing corn all day
—you looked so beautiful—
take the whetstone from me, lay it by the fire,
lead me, tiptoed, past our sleeping child
and fall asleep upon me, curls tickling my chin,
sweat-beads rolling from your shoulder-blades
into my mouth. Each time I swallowed one
you smiled and shivered in your sleep.

You've been a whetstone to my memory so long
it has grown hollow in the centre, like our sandstone step.

Acrobats

A somersault, a triple twist, a thousand sighs,
mirroring, in miniature, your long low glide
through spotlit shadows of the upper tent:
but only I can see your smile,
eyes closed, hands stretched towards my grip.

Gaping faces, a pale sky far below,
the screams, ionospheric static.
The tent breathes: we nestle in its billows.

When you whirl, hair streaming,
from the chain between my teeth,
the crowd sees a spinning sheaf of gold:
to me, you're circling, aching,
as we nibble to each other, link by link.

We bathe our skins
in the breeze from our close passages,
a leaf's-width separation, no more.
If we touched—however lightly—
we'd spin apart, out of control.

At dusk, tent empty,
weightless at the top of those great arcs,
we see stars below us,
studding the canopy's faint dome.

If river-mist creeps in,
swarms slowly up the mast,
spreads its cloak above the net,
we swallow-dance for hours:
no sound except our swooping,
no light except a violet moon—or sun—
the only shape, your face
suddenly upon me from all parts of the tent,
eyes open, breath skating on my skin.

Summer Solstice

(for Sharon Conlin)

Our shadows tug us up the slope to Rocky Point,
spokes blur outwards from the hub. The old dog
lopes ahead, stirred by scents from the Divide.
Seed-pods swoop across the Moon's wide chest,
you wobble near the crest, stoop, breathe in.

Salamander slide across the lake. Touch of skin
each time we reach, exchange the shrinking leaf.
Smoke mixes with the fragrances of pine, settles
on our wine, our twenty-year-old boat, our jokes,
—our plenty. A cloud drifts across your throat.

Our shadows brake the descent from Rocky Point,
boulders, ruts, smoothed out by smoke. Your tent
soothes me, your face has sailed away. Aspen
shiver moonlight. The old dog glows. Its tail
is hosing fires that whirl throughout the night.

Gift

You've marked the place with grass so fine
it feather-frames each word, not hiding one.

It's left a trace of pollen here and there
between the lines your finger moved along.

The evening's slow pace, the shrimps and wine,
talk around the lake, all awkwardnesses gone:

and you made space for me to enter, share
quietness to rest your wounded months upon.

Pillow-touch, grey lace. Ripples of your spine
in low light that showed your breathing, shone

across your face into our easy warmth. A pair
of lovers, deep. Yet your eyes stayed stunned.

Your daughter's grace. The scent of pine.
'A gift she was', you said. Unfettered, fun.

May time erase your pain. And may her hair
light on your skin again: feather in the sun.

Rear-View Mirror

(i.m. Margaret Guery)

Gulls hover as we drag it from the car
—a mildewed trunk,
brass corroded, initials a pale scar—

swing it high onto the pile, retreat
as it bursts
and papers flutter, settle at our feet.

A photograph, curled edges: a youth
scared-smiling
in a suit. You stub it with your shoe,

flick it past a pram, a broken swing,
and as it swirls away
you shrug, 'The morning of our wedding'.

Twenty years crossed out, compressed
into a moment's spite,
a spinning face, initials on a chest.

As the engine scatters gulls, you stare
into the rear-view mirror,
wind your fingers deep into your hair.

The Sinuosity of Coastlines and Rivers

CARTOPHAGRAM. For calculating, exactly and instantaneously, in miles or by request in versts, the sinuosity of coastlines and rivers.
18/6d. *Army and Navy Stores Catalogue*, 1907.

It follows to perfection
tributaries of the Nile,
Seattle's drunken waterfront,
intertwining lakes that gape
in Leningrad's white nights.

An areal attachment (acres
alternatively, roods)
measures young girls flexing,
cracked castles on a beach,
rattle-space of pear-seeds,
caves in limestone cliffs,
blowholes thinly gasping
in craters of the moon.

It estimates reflections
of fir-trees in a pool,
even when chance breezes
pull the rug from underneath.
It gauges smiles and frowns,
the grimace of a child
who finds her painting
crumpled in the bin:
but not the shadows that flit
behind her eyes: shards
of coloured shells we trample.

Wind-Rider

A wave rears above a coral reef, plunges
through a thinning cloak of foam onto the rock
—and a droplet flung towards the midday sun
shrinks, concentrates in rising air.
A mile above the sea
a grain of salt takes shape in mother liquor.

It speeds generally west,
its lens imaging a seed subdued by frost,
a heron corkscrewing the thermal wind,
cruising upside-down to watch the stars.

Brought low by thunderstorm's cold spillage
it swirls into a canyon,
skates across the nostrils of a mule.

Dried in desert foehn
it mirrors only glints and flashes:
a gong beaten in the sun's low light,
axe-heads looping on a mountain-side,
icebergs clashing in the night.

Sucked into a cumulus,
scratched by cosmic dust,
it blazes into ice,
sprouts six corners,
cants, scintillates in subdued light.

Fully grown, a snowflake,
it tumbles from the cloud,
settles on a wave,
zig-zags for a while, floats free.
It melts slowly, corners rounding,
and loose all over
spills thinning tongues of brine to chill the sea.

From the Valedictory Lecture Delivered by the Distinguished Cosmologist Professor Dr Franz-Josef Klemp to the Astronomical Society of the University of Bonn, December 20, 1982.

. . . while by death of the universe, my friends,
I mean the drift to uniformity within it,
a journey marked by explosions, stellar birth,
and once in a while, a flickering of green
from oceanic mists and the thinnest stratus
covering a young planet. Press a stethoscope
to space's frigid breast, and if you're calm
you'll hear it whistle, whirr and chatter
as cosmic rays criss-cross it. And perhaps
a hollow knocking from the furthest parts.

Could it be Suzanne? From Zanzibar or Mali,
some stretch of airless sand—full-length,
knocking with her fist, her failing strength,
against a tree? Her luck all drained away
after such a journey, the light and busy dark
she moved through, criss-crossed by wanderers
and quarks, strange scents and invitations:
seeking a new berth after she left me. Giddy,
listing, the tracks more tightly curving
than she'd thought: and finding what, my love?

The universe, like me, dear friends—like you,
perhaps—is sliding unsteadily downhill,
its order descending, lurching into chaos,
its purest forms of energy degraded to sullied,
spitting ones. A drunkard's path from anywhere
is always outwards—it can never be retraced.
A star, shrinking under gravity's long pull,
seethes under pressure to a new ignition point,
flings its temper to the frontiers of space,
pulses, bellows—but can never swell again.

At first we were careful, each word and pause
in place, each journey we took, thought out:
insipid even, except that we were thickened,
flavoured by our gravity, our steady burning.
Good to learn to loosen, frown or disagree,
see sweat-pools deepen, spread under your arms.
But each month, you undid another button,
I tightened mine to choking, could not breathe
or focus. Slattern, prude, we spiralled apart,
riding opposite arms of our emptying nebula.

Let us swing, link by link, along the chain.
Newton, grey-faced, sucks on cosmic dust
until the stars are born. Einstein, kneeling
at the centre of each one, nibbles them away,
breathes sunlight out. Leaves on planets
swallow it and grow. In wintertime they fall,
and as they're trampled, murmur a faint warmth
that trickles out to space, stretches, thins,
sinks into a coldness without shape or change.
In the universe's coffin, white dwarves spin.

Is that what happened; we swung along too fast?
In the orchard, when I wouldn't let you dream,
or that hazy meadow, when all you really wanted
was to doze with me; in that drifting boat,
when I grew jealous of your motionless horizon
and disturbed it. Each time, I was tugging you
from link to link, until I'd rushed you through
all stages it was good to share. Too late then,
my love, that I began to understand. Despite
my white-dwarf howls, you had to burn elsewhere.

As I pause, friends, restoring what nervousness
has sponged from me, consider cosmic scales.
This glass I raise to Galileo holds more atoms
of H2 than in a million cubic miles of space:
I sip perhaps a hundred thousand miles' worth,
and that moment before its moisture registers
reminds me of the interruptions in our chain:
how galactic spin protects it from collapsing,
how our bodies are pale bottles in which sunlight
is preserved for three score years and ten, or so.

In deep coma: yet from time to time he'd surface,
turquoise sky behind a shredded nest of cloud.
But those few moments—once again my father,
though I was not his son—were interruptions
to the new regime he'd entered, his world now
not those wild and awful flashes, eyes wide-open,
blind. 'A goose!', he kept on calling, and once,
'Strap him to the cart'. No. It was the silences,
where he was young again, no movement at all,
except once a quiver at the corner of his mouth.

Our astronomers define the universe's limit
as the point past which telescopes are blind.
When I heard that, my friends, fifty years ago,
its arrogance appalled me, I almost walked away.
But today, it seems a reasonable, humble view.
The bounds of each lost one of us are as far
as we can reach—they can't be more. Yet often
we don't know our visions. Hair keeps growing
after death. Swing the telescope right round!
Are we at the centre? Was the old priest wrong?

No limits to the chaos of the traffic buzzing
in the valleys between stars. When Queenie died,
and my father found me sobbing in the field,
he didn't understand how I could make her better
by breathing in her mouth. 'She's up there, son!'
He was pointing to the sky. My tears multiplied
the stars. Then I saw her, poised to spring.
I blinked again. She'd rolled onto her back.
Again. Again. She was scampering—restored.
And I saw that motion is a magic lantern show.

Stars, pulsar sources at the telescope's horizon
are receding at the speed of light. Messages,
however shrill, cannot travel faster. Beyond,
we can never learn about. So, 'Abracadabra!',
it doesn't exist, my soon-to-be-departing friends.
More arrogance, perhaps? Those twins in Adelaide
and Stoke, whose stabs of pain were simultaneous,
might think so. Yet, light can loop the world
in much less than a second, less than the time
they took to clutch their breasts and shudder.

My messages to you haven't changed, Suzanne:
they never will. But the meaning may have rusted
as you meandered south. You can't find them,
I imagine, in your tired mind's rumpled pockets,
but as the foreground fades—when you are dying—
when time and space have shrunk into a lilac point,
will their passions overwhelm you once again?
Will they dazzle you, my love, like those bubbles
from your clay pipe, more than sixty years ago,
or those spinning wooden beads, from even earlier?

Waves that come direct from stars, or bounce to us
from planets, bring stories of how it used to be.
Distorted, often, in whispers so weak, modest,
they might be one's own breath, only vague shapes
can be discerned. Yet their truth remains forever;
ferns inside a casket, bodies resting in the peat.
Tales from distant parts are oldest, posthumous
—dry screams issued at extinction, long before
our earth. While someone peering down at us, sees
mammoths graze; faint cracks widen, fill with blue.

Whisper me your story, I'm straining hard to hear.
I shouldn't need to know how the first sip tasted
as you rested at the well, or if the handle
was still slippery with weeds. Sufficient, surely,
that you went alone and stared into the black.
Will you hear me, love, as your camel circles,
slopes towards the hollow? A breath, at most,
hard to distinguish from the swish of hooves
in sand—but enough, I think, for you to falter,
shake your head, spit into the past, ride on.

I repeat, my cherished friends! There is no loss
of information. It travels on forever, intact.
What we can't do is retrieve it, if it's passed
beyond our niche of space and time. Its integrity
depends on never being found, for everything
we see or touch, we alter. Quanta flick the moon
to read its story—and the old man winces,
recoils. The earth leaps up to falling apples.
Andromeda's red shift is scarlet underneath.
It is holy only on the dark side of the moon.

Is that how I altered you, Suzanne: by spying?
At my bedroom window throughout the afternoon
as you picked raspberries? On your bowed head,
a knotted handkerchief. Softening your shape,
the smock you said would see you through. Fruit
in your basket was swelling, deep. You held
each berry as if you were in church, laid it
like a wreath. At times, you'd toss one high
and swallow it. Such impertinence! Such grace!
Then you felt my gaze, bit your lip to bleeding.

Listen to me, you shuffling, press-ganged youths
in the back row. You should not be here—better
in forests, dusk, places I never knew when young
because my telescope was always pointed at the sky.
Such purity up there, planets' edges crisp against
the void. Fifty years to learn that the purity
that matters most is often blurred—and anyway,
the edges breathe. Our hope must be to focus back,
love not Archimedes—he is safe enough—but women
lost in childbirth, babies left out on the hill.

Some cosmic names: Elinor, grey sweep of the rings
of Jupiter, soft folds of my mother's skirts;
Zachary, shooting star, fussing in a passive sky;
Helen, soft light in between. But not Suzanne:
warm bread, blankets, distant bees. Would it all
have been different if your name were Ruth or Mary?
Are you here tonight, my love? If I cup my hands
and roar, will you hear me? The tragedy, it seems,
is not so much forgetting as outgrowing memories.
Useless to remember now, your need for silences.

It's strange, friends, that as my eyesight falters
I begin to see. If I lie back and close my eyes
I can pierce this great hall's rafters, slates,
the ivy, stratus; reach beyond the sleeping sun
—and scarcely straining—Orion's stunted woods
to a phosphorescent chamber, the sheaf of light,
clear water, Blake saw in his visions, Einstein
found too thrilling to forget: and every child
has always known was there. I'll loose my collar,
splash it on my throat. I'll plunge my face in it.

Why are they applauding? I've not finished, yet.
Why are the Rector and the new professor rising
from their chairs, instead of resting in the pool,
drinking stars, like me? Why don't they disperse
to the madeira, port, whispered talk on tiptoes
in hitched-up gowns? Let me be, my friends! Here
there is no draught, and if I tap with my knuckle
I might hear a faint reply. They walk towards me
with white smiles. Behind them, Queenie settles,
crouches—ready—in a pale-grey, darkening sky.